Breath

of

New Life

Dearna,
May God bless
you with new life
every day
Fritz Mutti

EIGHT
MARKS
OF
SPIRITUAL
LEADERSHIP

FRITZ MUTTI

ABINGDON PRESS / Nashville

BREATH OF NEW LIFE

Scripture quotations are from the *Holy Bible: New Revised Standard Version*, copyright © 1990 Graded Press. Hymn references are taken from *The United Methodist Hymnal*, copyright © 1989 The United Methodist Publishing House.

This book is printed on acid-free paper.

Library of Congress Cataloging in Publication Data

Mutti, Fritz, 1938-
    Breath of new life: eight marks of spiritual leadership / Fritz Mutti
        p.   cm.
    Includes bibliographical references.
    ISBN 0-687-07564-5 (pbk. : alk. paper)
    1. Christian leadership--Methodist Church.   I. Title.
BX8349.L43M88   1999   98-49922
253--dc21   CIP

99 00 01 02 03 04 05 06 07 08 —10 9 8 7 6 5 4 3 2 1

MANUFACTURED IN THE UNITED STATES OF AMERICA

Contents

Acknowledgments

T HESE PAGES BEGAN as seeds planted by the spiritual leaders who nurtured me in the faith through successive stages of life's journey:

My parents Fritz and Phyllis Mutti, and my sister Sue Mutti Sonner, who surrounded me with love and encouragement during my formative years.

My beloved spouse Etta Mae, whose remarkable ability to listen and discern always challenges and sustains me; and our sons Tim, Fred, and Marty, who taught me how to live and how to die.

Pastors in a variety of settings, especially Earl C. Griffith, who modeled Christian faith for me during my high school years and helped me answer a call to ordained ministry.

Honored Bishops Eugene M. Frank and W. T. Handy, Jr., who provided me with spiritual leadership through their unique personalities.

Scores of wonderful teachers and mentors, among them W. Paul Jones, my instructor and spiritual director, who read the manuscript, offering insightful, and sometimes blistering critique.

A multitude of friends and colleagues whose names cannot be listed because of the space required, but who continually enable me to attempt spiritual leadership through my calling.

The seeds planted by those mentioned above blossomed when it became my privilege to deliver the Willson Lectures during Bishops' Week at Mt. Sequoyah, Arkansas, in 1996. I am grateful to all those who encouraged me to seek publication of the lectures.

Finally, I am grateful to those who may choose to read this material because they themselves want to be spiritual leaders in their own service.

Introduction

T HE RINGING TELEPHONE disturbed the few minutes of quiet I had enjoyed all day. "Fritz," said the person on the other end of the line, "this is Carmaleta Evans."

"Well, hi! How are you?" I responded, wondering what she wanted.

After a bit of chit-chat, she told me, "I am calling to invite you to serve as one of the adult leaders on the 1965 Mission Projects Tour."

I was honored that one with only two years of post-seminary experience would be invited to such a responsibility, so I quickly accepted her invitation. It turned out to be a life-influencing decision for me. That trip brought me to a deepened sense of commitment to Jesus Christ, and it opened my eyes to serious inadequacies in my ministry.

On that mission tour we visited more than a score of mission agencies. The itinerary included community centers, hospitals, retirement villages, schools, general boards, homes for children, camps, and social change organizations. Each one was unique, but a few had an excitement about them that inspired everyone on our bus. Why was that? The only thing I could put my finger on was leadership. The most vibrant, dynamic institutions reflected their leader's committed enthusiasm.

Still there was something more. Indeed, those persons exercised leadership, but it was leadership with a *plus*. They were more than men and women with a vision, more than competent administrators, more than effective managers. They were *spiritual* leaders, and that made the difference.

Those leaders I met on the Projects Tour could be identified as spiritual leaders because they walked with God and radiated an unseen power. Each one seemed to have a sense of divine calling. They believed that what they were doing was motivated by their faith in Jesus Christ. They cared for the persons they served out of their personal conviction that they had been accepted by a loving God. They motivated others to reach out for excellence, to risk failure for the sake of better ministry.

I was inspired by their witness and example. At the same time I was humbled. Clearly, their leadership contained a dimension that seriously was lacking in my own ministry. What is this *spiritual* leadership they exercised? Is it a gift others may receive? Could spirituality and leadership be bonded together in my life? Those questions have been with me now for more than a quarter of a century. They are to be the focus of these pages.

Some ten years after participating in that Mission Projects Tour, I was appointed to the conference council on ministries staff. This judicatory position afforded opportunity for participation in numerous high-quality leadership development experiences. All of those events helped hone my skills for ministry, but they did not overcome the continuing feeling that my ministry lacked a spiritual quality. There was little sense that I truly walked life's journey in the company of God. Worship had become an event I planned rather than something I experienced, prayer was left to crisis times, Scripture study led only to outlines for future sermons. My spirit did not sing with God's Spirit.

When I confessed the dryness in my soul to a small group of colleagues, they admitted suffering the same malady. So we created a spiritual-formation group in the hope that we could help each other grow in the Spirit. We read and discussed several books on spirituality. We identified some basic spiritual disciplines—prayer, Bible study, tithing, and sharing in groups—which we agreed to practice regularly. We asked for the gifts of the Spirit. All of us believed that church vitality had to be grounded in a spiritual renewal. We longed for that blessing in our own lives.

Several years passed, and those spiritual disciplines became part of my daily routine. Gradually, the covenant groups helped me cultivate a sense of the presence of God. Then, after eight years as a conference executive, in 1982 a new appointment took me, once again, to congregational leadership. As part of the get-acquainted process, I talked with members about seeking God's will and living in a discernment mode regarding every decision. One of my friends said this was just what the church needed. She even described me as a spiritual leader.

I was not convinced. In effect the spiritual disciplines had become, for me, another leadership tool. That was not the same thing as exercising spiritual leadership. My leadership seemed tied to methodology, not to my relationship with God. Could spiritual method lead to spiritual leadership? That was the question I was asking when I was appointed district superintendent.

During this period in ministry, the darkest night of the soul descended on our family. One evening our middle son, Fred, called to tell us he was in the hospital with pneumonia. "They are running some tests," he said, "to find out what kind of pneumonia it is." A few days later he broke the news to us that it was PCP—pneumocystis carinii pneumonia—one of those opportunistic infections associated with Acquired Immune Deficiency Syndrome. Fred was living with AIDS.

Four months later our oldest son, Tim, sent us a letter. "This is the hardest letter I have ever had to write," he penned. "I have to tell you that I have tested HIV positive."

Two of our three sons were living with HIV/AIDS. They faced almost certain death. For the next 40 months we rode the roller coaster of this terrible disease. Through tears we watched their bodies waste away. We ached as they encountered numerous hospitalizations; agonized when they endured hepatitis, tuberculosis, CMV, diarrhea, and dementia; despaired when, in the course of time, death took away their lives.

There was no way through that experience except by the way of anguished prayer. As Jesus found the strength to face Calvary through a prayer of sweat, blood, and tears in the Garden of Gethsemane, so we moved from sorrow to sorrow through suffering prayer. That prayer life led us into a new relationship with the Scriptures and a new awareness that God was with us in this terrible time. We began to live "in Christ," know his sufferings, trust his healing, hope in his resurrection. We became more open to the leading of the Spirit. Our experience was revealing the meaning of spirituality to us.

That journey through suffering helped move me out of a spirituality that was just another leadership method. It pointed me toward the source of vital spiritual leadership. I began to see that spiritual leadership is more than the ability to organize or inspire, plan or execute. It certainly is more than the addition of faith disciplines to those abilities. Spiritual leadership is more than human. It has a transcendent connection. It emerges when the total human experience communes with God. It comes from the deepest recesses of the soul, from the agony of loss, and from the pain of suffering.

At the same time it is an act of grace. God reaches out to human beings and enters into a genuine relationship with a person. Charles Wesley wrote about it: "I am thine," he sang, "and thou art mine." This is the meaning of spirituality. And spiritual leadership lives out of that relationship.

Spiritual Discipline of Being

After my election to the episcopacy in 1992, but before I assumed responsibilities in the Kansas area, I sought spiritual direction from several trusted mentors, including Bishops Reuben Job and William Boyd Grove, and my longtime friend, teacher, and guide, W. Paul Jones. Each one advised that immediate attention should be given to the creation of a spiritual rule or discipline that would undergird my service as a bishop. I knew that was important. But I also knew that it was about more than adapting an old practice to a new leadership setting. I longed to move beyond the knowledge of the source of true spirituality into a genuine spiritual relationship with the Holy One.

Paul Jones arranged for a retreat at Assumption Abbey, a Trappist Monastery located in the Ozark Mountains of southern Missouri. At the beginning of that experience, we talked about the long journey I had traveled in search of the meaning and experience of true spirituality. He described his own longing this way: "What are we to do with the longing for a 'more' that is 'beyond,' for a 'beyond' that is 'within,' for a 'within' that is 'all,' and for an 'all' that insists upon remaining 'mystery'?"[1]

For three days I enjoyed the solitude of a hermitage, while I prayed for a new understanding of calling, a clear vision of the results I hoped to attain in my episcopacy, a transforming spiritual discipline for my ministry, and the gift of vital spiritual leadership. I sought a self-understanding that was grounded in the Holy, a vision of leadership empowered by the Spirit, a way of living formed by a relationship with God.

9

Henri Nouwen, in a book of reflections on Christian leadership, gives voice to this hope. "The Christian leader of the future," he states, "is the one who truly knows the heart of God as it has become flesh, 'a heart of flesh,' in Jesus."[2]

He suggests that this element of spiritual leadership will be acquired only through the discipline of contemplative prayer.

Through contemplative prayer we can keep ourselves from being pulled from one urgent issue to another and from becoming strangers to our own and God's heart. . . .

It is not enough for the priests and ministers of the future to be moral people, well trained, eager to help their fellow humans, and able to respond creatively to the burning issues of their times. All of that is very valuable and important, but it is not the heart of Christian leadership. The central question is, Are the leaders of the future truly men and women of God, people with an ardent desire to dwell in God's presence, to listen to God's voice, to look at God's beauty, to touch God's incarnate Word and to taste fully God's infinite goodness?[3]

My retreat was dedicated to this kind of prayer. During that time away, my spiritual directors encouraged me to give more attention to being than doing, receiving than giving. At the monastery, others were serving me as priests, praying for me and helping me learn how to pray. Through worship experiences, they pointed me toward God. By offering me the Eucharist, they enabled me to commune with Christ.

I kept a journal of my reflections during that retreat in a book that was given to my son Tim by his seminary classmate Patti Ryle Clay. She had given it to him for his birthday in 1990, just a few weeks after she learned that he was infected with the HIV virus, and after she had covenanted to be a part of a support group on his behalf. Her inscription read: "It's good to be back in each other's lives. Here's a place to record some of your thoughts and dreams."

Tim never wrote a word in that journal, but it became a symbol of spiritual connection for me. On the first page I scratched a note to Tim: "You never wrote anything here, just as you and I never wrote any of those letters we intended regarding your illness. So the pages are blank. I am going to use this journal to record my reflections on the experience here at Assumption Abbey. I will sense your presence with me."

This book focuses on spiritual leadership. I do not intend to suggest that I model it. I assume that all of us are pilgrims in search of the same gift. It is not my purpose to complete an exhaustive survey of the literature on leadership or spirituality. As should already be clear, I offer here one bishop's reflections on the importance of spiritual leadership for the Christian community as we move through this time of radical change. Drawing on my experience as a pastor, program executive, and as a district and general superintendent, I will attempt to describe the spiritual leadership which is so desperately needed. More than this, however, I offer with all the passion I can muster, the plea for a common journey toward spiritual leadership.

A great deal is being written and said about leadership. Likewise, many recent volumes address various aspects of Christian spirituality. These writings, speeches, and workshops urge the development of leadership qualities, or they call persons to a renewed investment in the spiritual life. Not often enough do we put the two together. The blending, the connection of these two, is just what is needed. The Christian community must raise up, deploy, and support spiritual leadership to serve God's mission in Christ. The revitalization of the church must begin in the spiritual life of its designated leaders. So in these pages we attempt to describe and claim the spiritual leadership needed for the church in the world in which we live.

The organizing principles for this effort stem from a remark made by one of my seminary professors, Samuel Laeuchli, one day in an advanced seminar. "Every generation," he said, "must choose what it will emphasize." That remark has haunted me for more than 30 years. If this is so, and I believe it is, then it may be possible to identify different emphases in spiritual leadership which Christians chose to underscore through the ages. I believe that it is possible to identify three broad categories of spiritual leadership the church has emphasized through the years. These are spiritual leadership for Community Formation, Community Reformation, and Community Transformation. Under these headings it is possible to discern eight historic emphases which amplify these general qualities. Here is an outline we will follow:

1. Spiritual Leaders in Community Formation
   Spiritual Leaders as Mission Evangelists
   Spiritual Leaders as Teachers

2. Spiritual Leaders in Community Reformation
   Spiritual Leaders as Priests
   Spiritual Leaders as Preachers
   Spiritual Leaders as Pastors
   Spiritual Leaders as Ministers
3. Spiritual Leaders in Community Transformation
   Spiritual Leaders as Prophets
   Spiritual Leaders as Visionaries

None of these titles is new. While catchy reformulations of roles may help us escape the trite and shop-worn terms of the past, I believe it is important to redeem these familiar titles and fill them with more vital content. Indeed these terms are drawn from the past precisely because no people ever moved into new realities effectively without a deep appreciation for what has gone before. We do hope, however, that viewing old terms through the lens of spiritual understandings and contemporary leadership concepts will enable us to fill them with new meaning appropriate for the times in which we live.

Part One:

Spiritual Leaders in Community Formation

THE ACTS OF the Apostles reports that the Spirit of God moved mightily among the saints to form the Church. By the power of the Spirit, the disciples of Jesus Christ were transformed from a group of defeated followers into a team of spiritual leaders for a powerful community of faith. United around a common table, these early Christians worshiped the God of salvation, prayed for each other, and shared their meager possessions to the extent that all had enough. From that Communion table they went forth to heal the sick, visit the prisoner, set free the captive, and confront the powers of injustice.

By fire, the Spirit forged a community of faith. The members named this new community "the Way" because they pictured themselves traveling a narrow road for a brief time until the return of Christ. Those who journeyed this "Way" served God as sovereign ruler. They undergirded their life together through faithfulness to the teaching of the apostles, to the fellowship, to the breaking of bread, and to the prayers. Because the people of "the Way" believed Christ soon would return, they focused on the imminent end of time and gave primary attention to invitation and incorporation, to direction and doctrine. Everything they accomplished was seen as a gift of the Spirit.

"The presence and activity of the Spirit in the church," write William Barr and Rena Yocom, "is always a gift of God's free grace. . . . Further, the Church has to acknowledge that the Spirit is not confined to the Church. For, as Scripture attests and as the Spirit itself demonstrates, the Spirit is God's creative and redemptive, life-giving agency and power at work in the whole of creation, forming and transforming the world toward the fulfillment of God's aim."[4]

We now look at spiritual leadership in this ministry of community of formation. First, we see how mission evangelists invite persons into the Christian community. Then we observe how those who respond are formed through the ministry of teaching-learning.

Chapter One:

SPIRITUAL LEADERS AS MISSION EVANGELISTS

Every COMMUNITY GOES through a time of formation. Prior to this, individuals lead separate and disconnected lives. Then a leader invites them to pursue a vision of life-in-common that is better than life-apart. During this time period, people come together around a uniting leader, belief, or purpose.

Many are invited. Among those who respond, some accept the invitation because they hear a word of hope. Others come because they perceive that a good thing is happening in the new community. Many follow the call because of the leader's vision and charisma. Under that leader's guidance, community is formed. As the sculptor molds the clay, shapes and details it, so the leader joins with others to create and cast a new and united people.

Jesus' Way of Forming Community

Jesus formed a community of disciples through a leadership inspired by the Spirit. His own sense of calling and mission was confirmed and empowered by the Spirit. At his baptism, the dove of God descended upon him and a divine voice declared, "This is my Son, the Beloved, with whom I am well pleased" (Matthew 3:17).

In the desert experience, Jesus wrestled with temptations to mold his ministry after the model of miracle workers and magicians. Through forty days of fasting, he committed himself to the worship and service of God. He emerged as a servant evangelist calling persons into a new relationship with the sovereign God.

Jesus walked along the Sea of Galilee and invited persons to follow him into abundant life as disciples. He nurtured those who responded through prayers and parables, healing and helping. He stood courageously in the face of injustice, and in his death he demonstrated unconditional courage and love.

Jesus commissioned the first disciples to form faith communities through mission evangelism. Sent by Christ into the villages and cities, first they announced the good news that the reign of God was breaking into the world. Second, in Jesus' name they healed the sick, fed the poor, and provided clothing for those who had nothing to wear.

After Jesus' death and resurrection, the disciples went through a period of grief and despair. Then the Spirit came anew and anointed their leadership with power and vitality. Again they went out as mission evangelists to call persons into life in Jesus' name. This time they went in the name of the Christ who defeated death, and with the assurance that he was with them. C. B. Hogue wrote, "Witnessing is an overflow of the Christian experience. A Christian witness bubbles up, spills over, bursts forth. It is the product of life with Christ."[5] Surely that is what happened to the disciples. Formed by the Spirit of Christ, they went out telling good news and uniting persons in a community of witness.

Both Mission and Evangelism

In the company of Christ, disciples also create community through mission evangelism. How it happens is something of a mystery. At a global mission event, Heather Elkins compared this ministry to the wonder of the lodestone:

> The stone is dark, dull in color. It sits passively on a shelf, having little to commend it. It would not be picked up by children. It would be overlooked by those who like sparkle and shine. But pass it gently over a scattered pile of paper clips, and they vibrate and then seemingly leap

through the air and attach themselves to the stone. In places of chaos, order emerges. Separateness is drawn into unity. The lodestone, one of nature's natural magnets, has done its work.[6]

For nearly a century, our practice in Western Christianity has been to separate mission and evangelism. Advocates of mission seek community formation in the world. These witnesses believe the Church is called to lose itself for the sake of the world. So the emphasis is on apostolic ministries of service and justice, and the aim is a transformed world through prophetic witness.

Proponents of evangelism, on the other hand, hope to create community by drawing persons into the church through conversion and confession. As persons unite with the body of Christ in increasing numbers, the society itself is transformed.

Sometimes proponents of each emphasis are able to acknowledge the validity of the other. Too often, however, impassioned defenses of either mission or evangelism alone lead to division and name calling. The spiritual power of the Gospel is lost on numbers games and social action schemes. We cannot see the necessity both of evangelism and mission for genuine faith community formation. A church that uses only part of the spiritual power God offers it cannot be the faithful witnessing people Christ wants.

Bishop K. H. Ting of China declares, "Evangelism not only brings Christ to men and women—it brings Christ out of them, so that people at both ends of the line of communication are receivers of the gospel."[7] Genuine Christian community formation requires the rejoining of evangelism and mission in this kind of two-way thrust. A renewed spiritual leadership can help to make that happen.

Roger Swanson sees a model for that leadership in Jethro, the father-in-law of Moses. Exodus 18 tells how Jethro came to visit the Israelites after they had left Egypt, crossed the Red Sea, and begun their journey toward the promised land. Jethro was proud of Moses and gladly watched him exercise his leadership, but he wondered, "Why do you act all by yourself, Moses? This is not good. You and the people with you will wear yourselves out, for the thing is too heavy for you. You are not able to perform it alone." Swanson observes, "In a word, Jethro says: 'You are not leading God's people. You are letting God's people lead you!'"[8]

Jethro advised Moses to do three things: First, he was to represent the people to God through the spiritual ministry of prayer. Second, he was to teach the people what God wanted them to do. Third, he was to choose able persons as partners in ministry.

Jeannie Jenson, a pastor in eastern Kansas, is giving that kind of leadership in a growing congregation located on the edge of the metropolitan area. She effectively links mission and evangelism through the spiritual leadership she provides. She knows that persons cannot grown spiritually without regular participation in meaningful spiritual disciplines. She also knows that "going to church" seldom leads to spiritual growth unless that experience is linked to some opportunities for hands-on participation in mission projects. Leading her congregation out of its building into the community, she urges a missional evangelism that not only invites, but also serves the needs of persons. As pastor and people reflect on their efforts, they have been searching for ways to measure the effectiveness of what they do, and they have been developing new ways of measuring the results of ministries.

Spiritual Discipline of Witness

Leonard Sweet labels what I call mission evangelism as "hospitality evangelism." This occurs, he suggests, in three "I" stages: invitation, introduction, initiation. "Each one of these stages in ancient hospitality incorporates one of the three essential ingredients in postmodern evangelization:
invitation, *diakonia* and humble service;
introduction, *kerygma* and proclamation;
initiation, *koinonia* and community."[9]

Leaders needed for Christian community formation through mission evangelism will always seek to walk humbly with God. They will listen for the voice of the Spirit to guide them, and they will give themselves as servants so that the community may be strengthened. They will lead others in service and invitation because of their relationship with the risen Christ. His spirit, touching their spirits, will be their compelling force.

Those who live out of a Wesleyan heritage often sing their faith. Believing that things of the spirit may best be expressed in song, we bear witness through hymns of every kind.

Charles Wesley's great invitation hymn, "Come, Sinners, to the Gospel Feast" (339), provides just such a witness.

> Come, sinners, to the gospel feast;
> let every soul be Jesus' guest.
> Ye need not one be left behind,
> for God hath bid all humankind.
>
> Sent by my Lord, on you I call;
> the invitation is to all.
> Come, all the world! Come, sinner, thou!
> All things in Christ are ready now.
>
> Come, all ye souls by sin oppressed,
> ye restless wanderers after rest;
> ye poor, and maimed, and halt, and blind,
> in Christ a hearty welcome find.
>
> My message as from God receive;
> ye all may come to Christ and live.
> O let his love your hearts constrain,
> nor suffer him to die in vain.
>
> This is the time, no more delay!
> This is the Lord's accepted day.
> Come thou, this moment, at his call,
> and live for him who died for all.

Chapter Two:

SPIRITUAL LEADERS
AS TEACHERS

SPIRITUAL LEADERS ARE mission evangelists. They help form Christian communities by inviting people into new relationships of meaning and by joining them in service ministries in the world. Spiritual leaders are also teachers.

Formation occurs also as persons incorporate the sacred stories, core beliefs, and doctrines of the community into their lives. The ministry of teaching enables this formation process. Charles R. Foster states that the purpose of teaching "is to 'build up' or construct communities of faith to praise God and serve neighbors for the sake of the 'emancipatory transformation of the world,' which New Testament writers envisioned as the Kingdom of God. In this corporate educational effort the nurture of the faith and the practice of the witness of community members occur."[10]

A Teaching-Learning Community

The early church created a teaching-learning community, as well as an evangelical and apostolic community. Almost immediately the leaders discovered the necessity of teaching the core truths of life in Christ. When the anticipated return of Christ was delayed, the church gave increasing attention to the formulation of an apologetic. They invested energy in the defense of the faith against pagan philosophies and internal heresies. As successor to the Apostles, the Apologists attempted to develop a philosophical interpretation of the Way. At the height of this era, the great creedal councils were held, doctrinal unity was forged, institutional structure began to solidify, and the church became the guardian of the Truth.

The Church learned that a formed people must be an in-formed people. The word "inform" means "to give form to, put into form and shape." In his colorful manner, Leonard Sweet reminds us that the Church must have leaders who are

> in-formational connectors helping the body of Christ to become an in-formed church, and in-formational community. Informational communities exercise both informative and performative functions. The informative function is to impart ideas and to communicate concepts necessary for the life of the individual and the community. The performative function is to involve the hearers in the processes of information: to change attitudes, to inspire participation, to make good things happen.[11]

These teachers must be more than knowledgeable transmitters of information. Spiritual leaders who are teachers must also be persons formed through a personal faith relationship with Christ and moved by the abiding presence of the Holy Spirit. They must be persons so immersed in the continuing story of God's relationship to humankind that it is their personal story.

Spiritual Discipline of Study

Spiritual leaders are first learners, and then they are teachers. For the Christian community, learning centers in the study of the Scriptures. Richard J. Foster lists study as one of thirteen disciplines leading to spiritual growth.[12] Through the study of the Bible, people of God incorporate the story of God's saving history into their own being. The ancient story becomes the contemporary, molding, forming story.

Spiritual leaders also teach the faith. They can "shape and alter and elevate the motives and values and goals of followers through the vital *teaching* role of leadership."[13]

Today's secular culture pushes matters of faith to the edge of life. At the center of post-modern life rest self-reliant individuals, who make sense of life by collecting bits and pieces of truth from a data bank of experience. They then test this collected information by a scientific method modified in the laboratory of personal feelings. To a significant degree, these isolated individuals connect with each other through a materialist network of technology and acquisition.

Research confirms our observation that fewer and fewer people claim faith traditions as part of their own experience. Most are unfamiliar with the Bible, have little knowledge of the rites of the Church, and seldom participate in worship experiences. Rather than despair of our ability to relate to persons in this culture, Barbara Blaisdell chooses to see possibilities. She suggests that we offer spiritual gifts that resonate with this ethos. Among these gifts are understanding, empathy, and gratitude. Offering these gifts we may start where people are and challenge them to move beyond radical individualism. She invites us to recognize this generation's deep commitment to authenticity and self-fulfillment and its deep suspicion of external authority. She challenges us to begin with the gospel's power to touch a person's inner being, to offer occasions for direct service to others, and to invite participation in vibrant worship of the God who is imminently involved with life, but who also transcends it.[14]

Spiritual leaders choose to exercise the teaching function. "Teaching takes place because we have made a decision to influence what other persons may learn. When we teach we expect something to happen in the lives of students. We intend for them to appropriate information or concepts, deepen relationships, sharpen skills, change attitudes, make commitments or the like."[15]

Such teaching leads to authenticity, which in turn gives rise to empathy. Blaisdell notes how authenticity "requires a commitment to be aware of one's own pain and suffering, one's weakness and struggles with temptation."[16] Effective teaching can lead persons beyond themselves to empathy.

Experience-Based Teaching

Since the death of our sons, my spouse Etta Mae and I have shared our story of loss and grief dozens of times. We always try to put a face on HIV/AIDS by telling the story as personally as possible. We want those who hear to know that Tim and Fred, our sons, were real human beings who suffered through this devastating illness with courage and faith. We want folks to know about the physical pain. And we also want them to know of the social and psychological pain associated with AIDS. We tell about the fear, the rejection, the judgment, and the hostility that we encountered. Every time we tell our story, some listeners rise to the level of empathy in their response. They cry with us; they hug us; they want to know more; they offer to help others living with HIV infection.

We share this story, as teachers, confessing that our journey of pain and suffering was essentially a spiritual journey. Through it all, God was with us, encouraging us, and helping us to learn much of the divine nature and purpose. We believe that spiritual leaders in a renewed Church in the twenty-first century must have teachers who lead them out of depths of their personal encounter with God.

Part Two:

SPIRITUAL LEADERS
IN COMMUNITY REFORMATION

A FTER A TIME of formation, communities develop a shape and character. Then they enter a time of stability and a ripening toward maturity. Inevitably, however, changing contexts lead to a time of re-formation. Tom Sine describes it this way:

> We must unmask the powers in our lives, congregations, and the culture which have seduced us. We must be awakened to the reality that we are not called to advance the present order, but to be a part of the inbreaking of a radical new order. And essential to being part of this new order is the embracing of a new dream—a wild outrageous hope that the God who created all things will write the final chapter of the world and make all things new.[17]

The initial formative process in the Church took about three centuries. Then came the Constantinian edict, establishing Christianity as the religion of the Empire. In a very brief time, the situation for mission and ministry turned upside down. The once persecuted and derided church now received favor and privilege. During the next two hundred years, the Church adapted to its new status by taking the first steps of re-formation. These changes eventuated in the thousand year era of Christendom, but in the process, the Way was re-formed from a journey into a destination. The Church came to be viewed as an otherworldly Depository of Salvation.

Spirituality came more and more to be focused inwardly on the soul, and less and less outwardly on life in the world. Spiritual leadership coalesced in a clergy defined in priestly language. Priests performed religious rites in a realm separate from the real world. They meted out salvation through sacramental practice. They engaged in devotional practice on behalf of laity.

The flowering of monasticism constituted one of the most creative re-directions of the Middle Ages. When the Roman empire collapsed in the face of invading enemies, the spiritual leaders in these cloistered communities emerged as preservers of the ancient traditions and cultivators of a spiritual life that challenged the dualism of Church versus world, soul against body. The monastics sought to re-unite the spiritual and the temporal, for they knew that "spirituality is not a subdivision of Christian discipleship. It is the root, the source, the life."[18]

By the sixteenth century, changes sweeping the world accelerated, and the ecclesiastical hegemony started to crumble. Forces from myriad sources buffeted the Church. A fundamental re-orientation occurred during the Protestant Reformation. Of major importance was the reframing of leadership roles. The gap between clergy and laity was narrowed through an understanding of shared ministry in a priesthood of all believers. The roles of priest, preacher, pastor, and minister either emerged or were given new meaning and content.

In Part II we give our attention to these four leadership functions and attempt to discern their spiritual nature. When we add priest, preacher, pastor, and minister to the tasks of mission evangelism and teaching, we move further along in our quest for a comprehensive understanding of spiritual leadership.

Chapter Three:

SPIRITUAL LEADERS
AS PRIESTS

IF ONE OF the primary purposes of the Church is to care for matters of community re-formation, then the priestly office of leadership—through prayer, worship, and sacramental life—is a major component of spiritual leadership. The Church believes that God calls some persons out of the community of the baptized and ordains them for liturgical leadership. These spiritual leaders reform community through priestly ministry.

People everywhere seem dissatisfied with a life limited to the material and economic. Even the most secular publications observe folks on a spiritual quest. Feeling trapped by complex organizations they cannot change, and deluged by information they cannot understand, women and men search for an anchor in life. What they keep asking for in the Church is leaders who know God in Christ and who can help them experience the spiritual. They seek persons who are immersed in the disciplines of faith, committed to a transcendent cause, and who take seriously the life of worship and prayer.

It is this deep longing that these pages seek to address. But what does "spiritual" mean? More than a decade ago, William Stringfellow noted that it can refer to a wide range of practices:

"Spirituality" may indicate stoic attitudes, occult phenomena, the practice of so-called mind control, yoga discipline, escapist fantasies, interior journeys, an appreciation of Eastern religions, multifarious pietistic exercises, superstitious imaginations, intensive journals, dynamic muscle tension, assorted dietary regimens, meditation, jogging cults, monastic rigors, mortification of the flesh, wilderness sojourns, political resistance, contemplation, abstinence, hospitality, a vocation of poverty, non-violence, silence, the efforts of prayer, obedience, generosity, exhibiting stigmata, entering solitude, or, I suppose, among these and many other things, squatting on top of a pillar."[19]

Since that was written, we could add perhaps a dozen more fads which are labeled "spiritual." I have struggled mightily to come to my own definition of the concept. I find myself beginning with the connection between spirituality and spirit. Then I move to the conviction that it is focused on the connection between the divine, the holy, and our experience of life and its meaning. Therefore, the spiritual quest seeks a relationship between God's Spirit and my spirit, between the Holy Spirit and the community spirit.

Spiritual Discipline of Doxology

In the Church, leaders are ordained to guide persons in the spiritual journey. A priest serves God by keeping the community attentive to God,[20] and by leading in special liturgical acts, means of grace, which create a relationship between God and humankind. These are spiritual acts through which the Divine Spirit and the human spirit commune.

Christians affirm the biblical word that men and women are made in the image of God (Genesis 1:26). That is to say, that human creatures reflect the spiritual nature of God. "God is spirit," said Jesus to the woman at the well, "and those who worship [God] . . . must worship in spirit and truth" (John 4:24, NRSV). Prayer is possible because Spirit communes with spirit. Worship leads the creature into spiritual acts of adoration, confession of sin, thanksgiving, commitment, intercession, expectation, wrestling.[21] The sacraments celebrate God's mighty acts of salvation through the power of the Holy Spirit.

Christians are people who acknowledge that they belong neither to themselves nor to the age, but to God in Jesus Christ through the Holy

Spirit. They are out of step with a society that prizes individuality and autonomy. They are at odds with a culture in which power over persons and property gauges success and garners respect. Unlike their secular friends, Christians do not aim to be self-created or self-directed. Instead, they are directed by God, whose call to live a holy life dedicated to the rescue of others is laid bare in the life, death and resurrection of Jesus Christ.[22]

That powerful description by Ellen Charry points to God's intentions for humankind. Yet somewhere the image of God in human beings became tarnished and distorted. Not many live with such magnanimous altruism. We need to be made aware of our true identity through deeds of praise, remembrance, and community. It is the ministry of priesthood to lead the entire faith community in this spiritual task.

D. H. Tripp has identified several important elements of spiritual leadership in the worship life of the church.[23] One factor here is the way in which the pastoral ministry serves, on behalf of the community of faith, as a recognizable sign of the spiritual unity of the Church.[24]

Second, the personality and attitude of the leader affects the liturgical life of the church. Christian doctrine holds that the efficacy of the sacraments is never dependent on human faithfulness. Nonetheless, the people of God must see in the liturgist one who gratefully and humbly carries this sacred function with the utmost integrity.[25]

Third, leaders "exercise their function most properly in the pursuit of Christlikeness."[26] The one who seeks to help others worship, pray, and serve can do so most effectively when it is clear that that leader is living out of a personal relationship with Christ, when the leader is spiritually alive and growing.

A Covenant Community

Those called to the ministry of community reformation shape and re-shape the priestly office through spiritual disciplines, by sharing reflections on that journey with others, and through covenants of accountability in the quest. The leadership team of which I am a member has a group covenant to worship regularly, pray, study Scripture, fast, tithe, and serve. We see this rule of life as basic to our calling and necessary to personal growth in relationship to Christ and each other.

Those of us in the Wesleyan tradition do not use the word *priest* when we identify offices for spiritual leaders. Even so, Wesley constantly urged his Methodist friends to balance enthusiasm for good works by attending to the ordinances of God. In other words, he encouraged their priestly ministry.

He gave six counsels: . . . (1) Watch and pray continually against pride, against every kind and degree of it. (2) Beware of that daughter of pride, enthusiasm (defined as grasping for happiness without submitting oneself to its necessary preconditions; or as Wesley put it himself "expecting the end without the means"). (3) Beware of antinomianism (doing your own thing, regardless). (4) Beware of sins of omission (getting tired and supposing that what you've already done is plenty, or at least enough). (5) Beware of desiring anything but God. (6) Above all beware of schism, of making a rent in the church of Christ.[27]

A Sacramental Community

The celebration of the sacrament of baptism reinforces these disciplines within us. Every time a congregation marks a child, youth, or adult for inclusion in the community of faith through baptism, the commitment may be renewed.

After the General Conference of The United Methodist Church published a curriculum for the study of the sacrament of baptism, I offered to lead that study in every district, and in other places where time would permit. During the quadrennium I taught this course ten times. On each occasion we ended by celebrating a service of baptismal remembrance. Sometimes we poured water in a baptismal font and passed by, one by one, to touch the water and recall the meaning of our baptism. On two occasions we had fountains of running water that symbolized the living spirit of Christ, living and at work in our personal experience. Each time, all of us felt renewed spiritually as we opened ourselves anew to the indwelling of the Holy Spirit.

Baptism is a spiritual act by which persons are initiated into the body of Christ. A second spiritual act—Communion—nurtures and reforms the baptized community.

The movie *Places in the Heart* tells the story of a sheriff and his family living in a Texas town during the Depression. The film celebrates community in several different scenes. As the movie opens, folks are gathered for worship, singing "Blessed Assurance" and giving expression to one of the central tenants of our faith. Read over the words to this Fanny J. Crosby hymn (369), just to get a feel for the setting.

> Blessed assurance, Jesus is mine!
> O what a foretaste of glory divine!
> Heir of salvation, purchase of God,
> born of his Spirit, washed in his blood.
>
> This is my story, this is my song,
> praising my Savior all the day long;
> this is my story, this is my song,
> praising my Savior all the day long.

After church the sheriff, his wife, and their two children, gather at the dinner table and give thanks. The sheriff is called away to control a drunk who is down by the railroad tracks, threatening folks with a gun. He is an African-American man named Wylie. As the sheriff prepares to take Wylie to jail to sober up, Wylie's gun accidentally discharges and the sheriff is killed.

They take his body back home and stretch it out on that same table where the family had been eating their meal in peace. The sorrowing family surrounds their loved one. Outside, a mob hangs Wylie and then drags his body through the dust in front of the law officer's home.

In so many ways the film illustrates community being reformed around a table. As the movie comes to a close, the community gathers in church one more time. On this occasion they come around a Communion table, pass the bread and cup from person to person, and declare, "The peace of God be with you." And the words of the Gospel song echo in our ears: "This is my story, this is my song, praising my Savior all the day long."

It is a privilege to lead priestly ministry at font and table. When the spiritual leader comes again to these sacraments, he or she is reformed and enabled to help other persons find communion with Christ.

Chapter Four:

SPIRITUAL LEADERS
AS PREACHER

WITH THE FIRST murmur of God's call to yield my life in Christian service and vocation, I understood that God was calling me to be a preacher. After all, that is how we described the office of the leaders of our small-town congregation. They were preachers.

They were more than that, of course, but first and foremost they were preachers. In the Reformation tradition, where the Word occupies the center of faith practice, along with the Sacraments, preaching is a high and honored task. President Donald Messer of Iliff School of Theology writes, "Preaching, as understood theologically by the Protestant Reformers, is the work of the Holy Spirit. In Martin Luther's words: 'God speaks through the preacher. When we preach . . . we are passive rather than active. God is speaking through us and it is a divine working (that is happening).' "[28] Preaching is an expression of spiritual leadership.

Spiritual Discipline of Communication

There is no escaping the deeply spiritual nature of the preaching task. God calls spiritual leaders and gives the pulpit as a platform for ministry. As interpreters of the Word, who connect Scripture and tradition to present experience, preachers proclaim God's vision of the world's future. They inspire, encourage, challenge, confront, and teach. As preachers, they are about community reformation.

One of the first books on preaching I received as a young, pre-theological student had preaching as its subject. Written by Bishop Gerald Kennedy, it focused on the spiritual task of communicating the divine word to persons.[29] The chapter titles pointed to the awesome responsibility of speaking as God's ambassadors, "since God is making his appeal through us" (II Corinthians 5:20).

In another classic, which was required reading for my License to Preach, Halford Luccock wrote of the power behind the preacher. He told of an ordination preacher who pleaded eloquently for consecration of mind and energy, then ended up by exhorting the ordinands to "go out and give to your preaching all that is in you." That is exactly what preaching is not, Luccock insisted; rather, preaching "is giving that which is not in us at all."[30] Preaching channels the grace of God. As my beloved homiletics professor Merrill Abbey put it, "the Word interprets us."[31]

The preacher gets ready for the task by heeding the words of I Peter 1:14-15, NRSV: "Like obedient children, do not be conformed to the desires that you formerly had in ignorance. Instead, as he who called you is holy, be holy yourselves in all your conduct."

Through preaching, the spiritual leader enables the listeners to contemplate the holiness of God. Walter C. Kaiser Jr. writes in *The New Interpreter's Bible*:

> Because God is holy, God's people are to be holy by being like God in the world. We can, therefore, do away with all the cartoon pictures of the sanctimonious holy person wearing a halo and a prudish glare. To be holy is not to be narrow-minded and primly pious; it is, rather, to imitate God. To be holy is to roll up one's sleeves and to join in with whatever God is doing in the world.[32]

A Proclaiming Community

God uses preachers for the spiritual task of proclamation and invitation. There is both a joy and a burden in that duty. In a wonderful tribute to Gardner Taylor, "poet laureate of the pulpit," a *Christian Century* article tells of the sermon he preached to an audience of fellow preachers. Taylor spoke powerfully:

My brother preachers, you say that you want great power to move among men's heart strings? You cannot have that, without great sorrow. G-a-w-w-d can fill only the places that have been emptied of the joys of this life. . . . Now you may tickle people's fancies, but you will never preach to their hearts, until at some place, some solemn appointment has fallen upon your own life, and you have wept bitter tears, and gone to your own Gethsemane and climbed your own Calvary. That's where power is! . . . It is not in the tone of the voice. It is not in the eloquence of the preacher. It is not in the gracefulness of . . . [the] gestures. It is not in the magnificence of . . . [the] congregation. It is in a heart broken, and put together, by the eternal God![33]

When our sons Tim and Fred died of AIDS, my heart shattered into little pieces. God gathered up those pieces, holds them in a caring hand, and continues to mend this broken vessel. I may never be whole again, and I will never preach with the power of Gardner Taylor, but if there is any depth to my spiritual leadership, it is that sorrowful sackcloth that made it possible.

Word of Grace in Context

Once the preacher becomes an instrument of the Spirit, then it is possible to tend to the art and craft of proclamation. Preaching looks different in this electronic age than it did just a few years ago. A certain Peanuts cartoon strip shows Sally standing in front of the television set. A voice comes from a face on the screen, "Don't miss it! Be there!" Sally responds immediately, "Wait! Come back! I can't be there! I can't!"

She turns to Charlie Brown and shares her exasperation, "He said to be there! How can I be there? I don't even know what's going on! I can't just go anywhere! What does he expect?! I don't even know where I'm supposed to go!!"

"Look," counsels Charlie Brown, "you don't have to do everything they tell you on TV. . . .You don't have to believe all the things they say. . . ."

For three panels Sally ponders that statement. She turns to the set. She turns and looks the reader straight in the eye. She turns to the screen again. Then she whirls around and shouts to Charlie Brown, "You're kidding!"

Those who are called to preach today know what a difficult task it is. The authority an audience grants to the speaker no longer resides in an office. The message must come via a spiritually renewed person through a medium that post-modern people can understand and appropriate. God still provides grace sufficient for this task. The spiritual leader who is preacher proclaims good news and invites persons into a community of grace.

Chapter Five:

SPIRITUAL LEADERS
AS PASTORS

T HE REFORMATION OF the Church corresponded with a
massive reshaping of political and social realities accompanying the
demise of the Holy Roman Empire. State churches were established
according to the allegiance of the rulers. But other seeds were sown.
Some of those seeds sent up new shoots through the Radical Reformation, and they came to flower in a new climate.

In this historical expression of the Church, the concept of
covenant community came to the fore. The redeemed are an elect
community united to Christ in a spiritual unity.

Spiritual Discipline of Care

Spiritual leaders of covenant communities carry out their duties
with emphasis on the role of pastor. This understanding of leadership
comes from the biblical concept of shepherding. Alastair V. Campbell
sees that the shepherd leader in the Bible is "a strong and courageous
figure at the head of the flock. But this leadership has a very special
quality. Concern is entirely focused on those entrusted for care, even
to the point of life's surrender. Thus leadership is expressed in great

compassion, sensitivity to need, and a knowledge of what is life-sustaining and wholesome."[34]

Spiritual leadership is offered in this role through ministries of pastoral care. The pastor visits the sick and those imprisoned. She cares for those in sorrow and celebrates with those who know joy. He listens to the hurts of the people and counsels the troubled and lost.

A Community that Shares the Pastoral Task

One of the most compelling images of the pastoral role is suggested by Henri J. M. Nouwen in his book *The Wounded Healer.*[35] These pastors transform personal life struggles and scars into sources of healing and health. Indeed, true spiritual leaders find healing for themselves before they become healers who share the pain of the people in congregations and in the workplace.

The small United Methodist congregation where my mother holds her membership has lost nearly one-half of its members since 1960. The decline is a bit more severe than the decline in the city's population. Today there are perhaps 75 family units related to the church.

My mother knows that I have a deep interest in the life of the congregation. Through the years we have talked often about its health, and not infrequently the discussion has centered on spiritual leadership. Over and over, Mom has stated her hope that the clergyperson will be a pastor. "Now it is not necessary to call on me," she would say. "But it would mean so much if he could just drop by to see Helen, or Cleo, or Lily."

If Mom reflected the expectations of the larger congregation, there was not a lot of demand for leadership in mission, or Christian education, or administration, or community action. They wanted sermons that were not boring, but they did not have high expectations for homiletical excellence. What they begged for over and over again was pastoral care. It seemed they never got enough. Ministers came and went. The congregation continued to seek leadership with a sensitivity to the possibility of church reformation through pastoral care. They always asked for more pastoral visits in homes. Some ministers did not manage hospital calls very well, and one or two did not bother even to make a pastoral visit when there was a death in a family.

Maybe I am old fashioned, but I believe that Mom's congregation had a right to better pastoral care than they received. Even if physicians no longer make house calls, pastors should. Even if times have changed, it is still important to meet one another face to face in a time of crisis. It is still important to hold hands and share a word of prayer together. One cannot be a spiritual leader at a distance.

Surely it is not too much to expect that a spiritual leader with fewer than one hundred families should make at least an annual visit in every home. In addition, it would seem possible to visit every shut-in once a quarter and to contact every family by telephone on a birthday or an anniversary.

There is no contention here that a better job of pastoral care miraculously would turn the membership decline around. Much more is needed. But what if the leaders of our congregations saw pastoral care as an instrument for spiritual reformation in the church? What if clergy and laity decided to create a partnership in pastoral care? Teams of people, including the pastor, might be responsible for hospital, nursing home, and shut-in visits. A lay member might accompany the pastor when a death call is made.

Team members might share their own experiences of loss and grief before making the visit. In the process of telling of their own wounds, they might release the powers of healing for themselves and in turn for the persons they go to visit. Perhaps clergy would release their resentment of the laity's demands for pastoral care, and maybe the laity would begin to see that life in the church is the responsibility of everyone, not just that of the hired hand. As Henry Ward Beecher put it, "Compassion will cure more sins than condemnation."

Who knows? Maybe a church that cared about its members would begin to show the same care for persons outside the official roll. A caring congregation might even generate some contagion that would appeal to others. Worship might generate some excitement if participants cared about each other. Members might begin to live invitationally. Instead of just complaining that youth and young adults do not attend, a pastoral congregation might begin to design ministries that would meet the real needs of persons in those age groups.

In New York City, a woman from Harlem was honored for her compassionate care of children. When social agencies had called, she had taken the boys and girls in and provided a home. Most were literally off the streets; many of them had been abandoned by parents on drugs, and not a few had been orphaned by domestic violence. As she received the plaque, she leaned on her crutch and said, "I've had over 500 children in my little shack, and they tell me that they are different because of it—and as long as I can get to my door, I will answer any knock."[36] Leaders who see pastoral care as a part of vital spirituality just might start a genuine reformation.

Balance In Ministry

Now we need to remind ourselves that these same leaders need to plan for balance in ministry. In a church like my home congregation, it would be easy to major in pastoral care to the exclusion of everything else. A leader who listened to the pleas of the people could easily become a chaplain and little more. There may be about as many leaders who make the mistake of over-pastoring as there are leaders who do too little pastoral care.

This is just as devastating to a congregation. Spiritual leaders who overemphasize pastoral care end up paying too little attention to teaching, evangelism, stewardship, or outreach. In the state where I live, there are scores of pastors who provide marvelous care for individuals, but seem oblivious to the fact that the congregation is dying while they burn out.

Attention to the creation of a balanced pastoral ministry will help us look beyond individuals and congregations to the larger community. As life gets more and more complex, folks are tempted to turn inward. Americans, in particular, have always venerated individualism to the detriment of the common good. The goal of self-fulfillment too easily becomes selfishness. Our communities become fragmented, isolation sets in, and new residents are looked on with fear and disdain.

Once we begin to care for each other in the primary group of the congregation, it may be possible for us to reform our relationships in the work place. Observers note that the workplace is increasingly the chief place for people to find relationships and meaning. It is much more likely that we will have long-term connection with colleagues than we will with neighbors we do not know, or even extended family who may be living all over the world.

Leaders, who take pastoral care seriously, rightly see the spiritual nature of caring. Through ministries of care, God reaches out and touches persons, offering healing and creating relationships of love.

Chapter Six:

SPIRITUAL LEADERS
AS MINISTERS

IN THE WESLEYAN revival and other forms of evangelicalism, the stress is on the sanctified and holy life. The Holy Spirit empowers believers to live a godly life in which moral and ethical matters become paramount. The Word of Grace has been heard, and the covenant community seeks to act out its imperatives.

In communities of holiness, spiritual leadership is entrusted to a minister, who is responsible for ministry. My own denomination, The United Methodist Church, offers this statement about ministry:

> The heart of Christian ministry is Christ's ministry of outreaching love. Christian ministry is the expression of the mind and mission of Christ by a community of Christians that demonstrates a common life of gratitude and devotion, witness and service, celebration and discipleship. All Christians are called to this ministry of servanthood in the world to the glory of God and for human fulfillment. . . .[37]

Spiritual Discipline of Service

Leaders in ministry may be lay persons or clergy, but they give spiritual leadership through the service they render. H. Richard Niebuhr used the term *pastoral director* to describe the role of minister as I believe it is often used in the church. What he referred to was one who carries on all the traditional functions of the ministry: preaching, leading the worshipping community, administering the sacraments, caring for souls, organizing an office, and taking on coordinating and management responsibilities.

For most of my life, this has been the dominant image of leadership in the church. When we were not calling our clergy person "preacher," the title most often used was "the minister." The task of ministry has been refined and perfected over and over in this age of corporate modeling. Skillful ministers have contributed much to the continuing re-formation of the church. But even though this role encompasses many of the elements of spiritual leadership we have identified, it cannot stand alone. It especially neglects the formational and transformational roles of mission-evangelism and teaching, of prophecy and visioning. There also is the tendency to see ministry in professional, methodological terms. We are looking for skilled administrators and change agents, but more than this, we are looking for ministers who involve themselves in the organizational life of the church because they are "free toward it" and do not "cling to it with a destructive possessiveness."[38] We are longing for ministers who can synthesize outward action and inward contemplation in the perspectives of hope, receptivity, and shared responsibility.[39] We are looking for leaders who practice the spiritual discipline of service.

A Community to be Managed and Administered

"Leadership," writes Lovett Weems, "is often confused with administration and management. Administration is doing things right. If there is a deadline, one meets it. If there are stated policies, one keeps them. Management is doing the right things—such as planning and setting priorities."[40]

While leadership is not the same as administration or management, it does include these two. We urge a spiritual leadership in which one of the component parts is ministry through reformation.

Management is one expression of ministry. Let us consider this task first since it is more important first to choose the right thing and then to do it the right way.

The starting point is a leadership that relates to God in a discerning mode. It seeks change and re-formation discerned as God's will in Christ. This ministry is deeply spiritual, for it arises from the ongoing search for a divine purpose in relation to human need. Inagrace Dietterich writes:

> If attention is given to the processes of decision-making within the church, it is usually viewed as an organizational rather than a theological concern. . . . Discernment is a process of sorting, distinguishing, evaluating, of sifting among competing stimuli, demands, longings, desires, needs, and influences, in order to determine which are of God and which are not. To discern is to prove (test) "what is of the will of God—what is good and acceptable and perfect" (Rom. 12:2). Thus the goal of decision-making in the church is not simply to discover the will of the community, but together to discern the will of God.[41]

Administration is another expression of ministry. The two words come from the same root, which means "to serve." Jesus showed the kind of ministry he wanted his followers to practice when he knelt before each of his disciples individually, took a basin of water, and washed their feet. Earlier, when James and John had asked for places of special recognition among the disciples, Jesus had instructed them, "Whoever wishes to become great among you must be your servant" (Mark 10:43).

The Minister as Steward

Spiritual leaders let Christ-like service characterize their work. Peter Block's excellent book *Stewardship* is all about choosing service over self-interest. He writes about leaders who are stewards.

> Stewardship holds the possibility of shifting our expectations of people in power. Part of the meaning of stewardship is to hold in trust the well-being of some larger entity—our organization, our community, the earth itself. To hold something of value in trust calls for placing service ahead of control, to no longer expect leaders to be in charge and out in front.[42]

This spiritual leadership expresses itself in relation to management and administration concerns. Block continues, "There is pride in leadership, it evokes images of direction. There is humility in stewardship, it evokes images of service. Service is central to the idea of stewardship."[43]

In a less elegant metaphor, William Abernethy compares this ministry to a junior high youth group car wash. "The way to deal with the man with the muddy shoes is to invite him out to the church driveway and then 'baptize' him with sponges, buckets of soapy water and hoses of running water. All done while we, the washers, along with him, are sopping wet and getting wetter. And done with laughter, playful laughter. Muddy shoes are serious, painful business. But washing off the mud need not be."[44]

A basic ministry of the Christian community is to build up the body of Christ. The Church is re-formed when leaders help the community grow. In recent years theorists encouraged leaders to be about this duty through enabling ministry. We put it this way: The clergy are set aside to equip the laity for their ministry. There was merit in the concept, for it helped laity to assume responsibility for ministry. At the same time, it created an elitist clergy that saw its role as something different than doing the ministry. A better model is that of Jesus, who gives up all privilege and engages in servant ministry with the disciples.

This kind of spiritual leadership resonates with the current emphasis on quality. Such ministry discerns God's will and attempts to do the right thing in the right way. It offers itself in Jesus Christ and for others. It desires excellence in all things.

Part Three:

SPIRITUAL LEADERS IN COMMUNITY TRANSFORMATION

In OUR INTRODUCTION we offered the idea that every generation of Christians must decide what to emphasize. For the early generations, those decisions led to emphases that helped form the people of Christ's way into a spiritual community. In Part I, we considered the leadership roles needed by the Church in order for it to fulfill its spiritual ministry of community formation. The two roles we discussed were mission-evangelist and teacher.

When the Emperor Constantine converted to Christianity and by edict established the Church as the official religion of the empire, it became necessary for the community of faith to take a new look at Paul's word to the Romans (Chapter 12, verses 1-2). The Apostle's words came alive for them: "I appeal to you therefore, brothers and sisters, by the mercies of God, to present your bodies as a living sacrifice, holy and acceptable to God, which is your spiritual worship. Do not be conformed to this world, but be transformed by the renewing of your minds, so that you may discern what is the will of God— what is good and acceptable and perfect."

The church had to struggle with changing circumstances. It was clear that the people of God were in danger of being conformed to the world. It could be said that the Church was the world. Were church members ready for transformation? Were they ready to be changed again into an entirely new substance? Clearly they were not. The operative mode was re-formation. It was easier to make adjustments that would result in a new conformity than to be open to total transformation.

In Part II we discussed the impact of spiritual leadership as carried out in four different roles or emphases. Then we examined their impact in the re-formation of the church. When we spoke of priests, preachers, pastors, and ministers, we dealt with familiar images, used and adapted by the church, that most of us have known throughout our lives. In that section, we noted the importance of linking those four roles with the formational leadership tasks of mission-evangelist and teacher in order to create a comprehensive and balanced spiritual leadership.

I feel a considerable satisfaction with this conception of ministry. And yet I cannot escape a high level of discontent. Will these tried and proven models be appropriate for the future we face? I cannot believe they will be enough. Can they be redeemed for truly spiritual leadership? Yes, they could be. And that is what we are about in these lectures.

Professor Darrell Jodock offered comments on the lectionary lessons from Jeremiah, I Corinthians, and Luke used in the winter/spring of 1995. He wrote:

> The people in seventh century Judah and first century Nazareth needed a prophet. They were ready for minor reforms and for wonderful deeds, but they *needed* a prophet. [Today] there are voices urging us to reform our public lives and move away from the idolatries of the present age. But we need a prophet, someone who will call us to a fundamental reorientation of individual and national priorities. We too are content with external reforms and not ready to confront the darkness in our own character. We want a future based on familiar premises even if they are no longer working. We still want to find our solutions in more education and technology, find communal well-being in more individual freedom, derive economic security from competition unbalanced by social concern, and acquire abundance through environmental exploitation. But disillusioned Americans drift without direction while an uncivil discourse born of frustration, disappointment and confusion grows more shrill and more disparaging. We urgently need a reorientation.[45]

Just a cursory observation of the world in which we are called to be the community of love indicates that we must heed Paul's words in our time. These are days in which we must submit our lives for transformation. It will not be enough to make adjustments, to tune up the old systems, to improve the quality of ministry as we have always lived it. Jim Wallis writes:

> The world isn't working. Things are unraveling, and most of us know it. Tonight, the urban children of the world's only remaining superpower will go to bed to the sound of gunfire. Bonds of family and community are fraying. Our most basic virtues of civility, responsibility, justice, and integrity seem to be collapsing. We appear to be losing the ethics derived from personal commitment, social purpose, and

spiritual meaning. The triumph of materialism is hardly questioned now, in any part of our society. Both domestically and globally, we are divided along the lines of race, ethnicity, class, gender, religion, culture, and tribe, and environmental degradation and resource scarcity threatens to explode our divisions into a world of perpetual conflict.[46]

In similar times, when the world waited on the brink of such pervasive metamorphosis of old forms, God raised up prophets and visionaries who hammered out a framework of possibility and hope. We stand in need of spiritual leaders today who can point to the rule of divine justice and announce a "new heaven and a new earth," under the reign of God, where a transformed humanity will reflect the incarnate love of Christ for the entire creation.

Chapter Seven:

SPIRITUAL LEADERS
AS PROPHETS

ONE OF THE gifts which a transforming community of Christians in the Latin American church shares with the world is the dream of liberation. Numerous books explicate the hope. However, it is through real persons living prophetic lives that the idea takes on form and power.

Archbishop Oscar Romero, a fairly ordinary priest, went through the motions of a rather common ministry until he began to know the poor of his diocese as human beings. Those fellow pilgrims suffered immense personal pain and collective injustice at the hands of the political rulers of El Salvador. One day Romero began to see that his spiritual mission was to stand with these children of God in their trials. His witness generated a power few expected, and it provoked the anger of governmental authorities, who warned that Romero's life was in danger if he persisted. He was not deterred. Hundreds of unnamed peasants were already dead or had disappeared, and their sacrifice inspired him. One day while he stood at the altar, offering the worship of the people through the mass, soldiers gunned him down with a torrent of bullets. Romero's death linked him in a partnership of martyrdom with scores of others and kept the liberation hope alive. Because of their prophetic witness, others in El Salvador and every country now know the world is on the edge, waiting to be transformed.

Less than a decade ago, the situation of black South Africans was so desperate that few believed apartheid would ever be dismantled. I was in southern Africa in 1988 with a mission education team. Among the people we met were Abel and Freda Hendricks, committed Christians who served Christ through a congregation in Cape Flats. Abel Hendricks responded to a call to ministry with the supposition that he would give leadership to the church as a scholar. The proud holder of a Ph.D. from Princeton, Abel returned to his country expecting to settle down in a nice little parish where he could read and write. But, the church sent him to the Cape Flats, a desperate community of persons disenfranchised by the racist government of South Africa. There he began to identify with the people of his community. He told us how worship pointed the people to a saving God. He showed us a candle, which served as one of the symbols that emboldened the people in the face of violent repression. In all ways but one, it was like a million candles in thousands of other churches. But what made this candle different was the strand of barbed wire that encircled it. Abel Hendricks said, "We know that we live in a dangerous, unjust society. The barbed wire reminds us of that. But we also know that the love of God shines through that injustice. When we light this candle we are able to see the light of hope in spite of the barbed wire of hatred."

Spiritual Discipline of Politics

A certain mythology colors our understanding of prophetic ministry. Seeing brave men and women stand up against tyrants, and watching them suffer abuse in the hands of hateful mobs, it is easy to conclude that the prophets are iconoclasts who leave everything they have known and been in order to enter a new age of hope and justice. It is more honest to say that they answered God's call the way they did because they were firmly planted in the spirituality of the Christian faith tradition.

What is needed in our time is the recovery and renewal of that tradition. Kenneth Leech points us toward a

> tradition that is open to the disturbing challenges from which renewal of life can come. Spiritual life stands always in need of interrogation by the

Word of God, of self-scrutiny and perpetual *metanoia*. It is a tradition that is never "at ease in Zion" but always restless, always struggling. It is a tradition of pilgrims and sojourners who are never fully at home in this world, never adjusted to the values and norms of any given order, but always seeking to be a community of contradiction and dissent, of scandal and prophetic testimony. It is a rebel tradition, a tradition of faithful and truth-seeking nonconformity, a tradition of sojourners in quest of a better city.[47]

B. D. Napier lists seven concepts of that faith tradition exhibited by the classical prophets:

1. "Thus says Yahweh;" Word and symbol
2. "Out of Egypt I called my son;" Election and covenant
3. "They went from me;" Rebellion
4. "They shall return to Egypt;" Judgment
5. "How can I give you up?" Compassion
6. "I will return them to their homes;" Redemption
7. "A light to the nations;" Consummation.[48]

Put those ideas together, and you begin to get a picture of the spiritual leader who is a prophet. Donald E. Messer's "political mystic" illustrates the concept.[49] This leader brings together prayer and social action, the religious and the political.

Many church leaders yielded to the temptation to separate the two in earlier decades of this generation. The result was a leadership given almost exclusively to political activism yet limited almost entirely to personal piety. The spiritual leader who is prophet will link these two energies for the sake of a church reaching out in service to the world.

A few of us in Kansas are making some feeble attempts at this through a roundtable organization we call "The Rural Religion and Labor Council." The idea is to get folks who profess religious faith in a variety of communions to peek into the future with colleagues from labor and agriculture organizations.

One of the issues we addressed was the North American Fair Trade Agreement. Organized labor felt threatened by the infusion of thousands of very low-paid workers into this enlarged market. Small farmers in particular foresaw their ability to survive further eroded by the potential strengthening of corporate agriculture. Many in our group feared that these apparently inevitable changes would so alter the social contract that thousands of persons would suffer terrible loss.

Our role in the struggle was to offer spiritual resources to our friends facing the very difficult changing realities. It is a spiritual leadership role that can make a difference.

A Community Engaged in Grief Work

Pastor and campus minister Phil Shull, one of the participants in our dialogue, reflected on that discussion in light of the threefold model of change that Alvin Toffler laid out several years ago. Toffler argued that culture has seen three major shifts or waves. The first wave moved persons from hunting and gathering to a structured and relatively stable, agricultural economy and society. In the second wave, society moved from farming toward industrialization. We now ride the third wave— "the transition from the industrial age to the high-tech, high-mobility information age. This new age has many names: post-industrial, post-modern, cybernetic globalism, the information age, etc." It is possible to view the first wave in terms of formation, the second as a time of reformation, and the third as an era of transformation. Phil Shull observes the following:

> Most of Kansas continues to work and live in a highly sophisticated version of the first wave. The values and work styles of rural Kansas have never really changed from the first wave to the second. Many folk assume otherwise. Meanwhile many of our, so called, urban dwellers are continuing to function in the second wave, while idealizing the first. A few of our folk, in all parts of Kansas are living and working within the third wave, while enjoying the lifestyle of the first and denigrating that of the second.

> The assumption has been that we are helping people move from wave two to wave three. In reality, for most of Kansas we are attempting to move people from wave one to wave three, skipping over all the cultural phenomenon of wave two entirely. Our mistake was to assume that as the economy made adjustments so did the cultural thinking as MTV entered our family rooms and fax machines were placed on the dashboards of our pick ups.[50]

During the past four years, several colleagues, both clergy and lay, suggested to me that creative grief work could be a very prophetic function. My first reaction was that this is a pastoral matter. Then I thought about the Old Testament prophets. As they lived out their calling, they helped people mourn the demise of the old. They put on sack cloth and sternly urged the people to do the same. Together, they lamented the passing of the old and prayed for healing. They also begged God for eyes open to the future and for transforming grace. For them, prophecy was a spiritual vocation.

Elijah, Elisha, Amos, and Hosea named reality for the ancient Hebrews. They let it be known that death and destruction were coming—indeed were already present. They pleaded for a willingness to turn from the past to a new day.

The spiritual leadership of prophetic transformation must help persons close the door on a past that cannot form or reform the future. Formation is needed for this generation, but it cannot be the same formation that enabled persons to live in an agricultural economy. Reformation can be appreciated, but bringing the unimaginable technology of the future to bear on the industrial mindset, as we already know, will only lead to grief. Indeed it is this cybernetic revolution that triggered the transformation in the first place.

Living Between the Ages

Prophets live between the ages. They walk the bridge from one era to the next. The Rural Religion and Labor forum helps us see that spiritual leaders for the next century may have to walk more than one bridge.

To get to the world-that-is-coming, some persons will have to move directly from a "rural" milieu directly to the information age. There is nothing to be gained by forcing this segment through the reformation of industrialization. They will need leaders who are able to help them go directly from first wave thinking to third.

Leaders will have to start in a different place with those whose world view comes from the industrial era. Among this community are not only the blue-collar folks of the labor movement, but also the white-collar people of the transnational corporations, including those in agribusiness.

Prophets stand ready to endure the displacement of these transformations. Moses wandered for 40 years in the wilderness with an exodus people. Jeremiah and Ezekiel went into exile with a conquered people. Jesus died on a cross.

That same Jesus rose from the grave and now works among his disciples to transform the world into the community God desires. As we follow him we sing in hopefulness. Charles Wesley's hymn of praise, "Rejoice, the Lord is King" (716), gives voice to our hope.

> Rejoice, the Lord is King!
> Your Lord and King adore;
>   mortals, give thanks and sing,
>   and triumph evermore.
>
> Lift up your heart,
>   lift up your voice;
>   rejoice; again I say, rejoice.
>
> Jesus the Savior reigns,
>   the God of truth and love;
>   when he had purged our stains,
>   he took his seat above.
>
> Refrain
>
> His Kingdom cannot fail;
>   he rules o'er earth and heaven;
>   the keys of earth and hell
>   are to our Jesus given.
>
> Refrain
>
> Rejoice in glorious hope!
> Jesus the Judge shall come,
>   and take his servants up to
>   their eternal home.
>
> We soon shall hear the archangel's voice;
>   the trump of God shall sound, rejoice!

Chapter Eight:

SPIRITUAL LEADERS AS VISIONARIES

T HE COSMIC UPHEAVALS of our time offer us few clues for discerning leadership emphases in the future. It may well be that the church of the twenty-first century will be a community of hope for persons seeking a new life of freedom. One thing we know is that God is sovereign ruler of the future as well as the past. Christ has gone before us into tomorrow to prepare a way for us. The Holy Spirit dwells among us to help and guide us into that new world emerging.

> The mission of the Spirit, in relation to Jesus, is to glorify, to reveal, to bring to remembrance, to witness, and to give life. In relation to the disciples and believers, the mission of the Spirit is to give witness, to teach, to remind, to guide, and to abide. And in relation to the world, the mission of the Spirit is to convince, to admonish, to illuminate and to judge. This power and guidance and this anticipated work of the Spirit, is behind and ahead of the disciples' mission in the world.[51]

Spiritual Discipline of Discernment

Spiritual leaders seek a vision of God in the contemporary world. They "speak of God and the deep things of the Spirit in ways that are meaningful in the present climate."[52] But it is not their initiative that matters. Rather, the Spirit dwells within leaders and gives vision for the future. In most religious cultures, persons said to be "in the spirit" are able to see the future unfolding. They are the visionaries.

One of the congregations I served as pastor threw itself into the arduous task of constructing a new building. They wanted to build a new facility where teaching and learning, fellowship and service could honor God. After two hard years at this project, the members were proud of the results. They had accomplished something worthwhile.

However, beyond that tangible result, something more important happened. The building program gave birth to a new vision of ministry which would carry that congregation into the future. The vision had not taken on flesh and blood yet, for visions are not fully formed programs. Rather they are sketches, outlines, and dreams.

The content of that vision paralleled the ministries that are described in the sixth chapter of Mark. In this passage we have a crescendo of events. First, Jesus visits Nazareth. Then, the 12 are sent on an evangelistic mission. That is followed by the death of John the Baptist and the feeding of the 5,000. Finally, the passage reaches a climax when Jesus is seen walking on water.

What goes into the vision of Jesus walking on water is the experience of discipleship. Following Jesus meant being an evangelist, a prophet, and a servant. When the disciples had done these things, they were able to see what others could not see. They were able to see Jesus walking on the water.

The leaders who guide us into the future will partner with others in ministry that gives rise to vision. According to Lovett Weems, "Vision is the single most common theme in leadership studies."[53] When asked to tell what vision is, Weems responds, "It is a picture of a preferred future."[54]

> Think of vision as that to which God is calling us in the immediate future. Visioning is not a simple undertaking. In retrospect, it may seem simple because the result appears so clear and obvious. Yet, the process which leads to the simple vision is often complex, intuitive, and spiritual. The route to a vision is rarely easy, direct, obvious, or uniform. It is helpful to remember that visioning is at its essence a process of discernment.[55]

Visionaries in the Church live in such close relationship with the Spirit that they are able to discern God's hope for the future. They lead others in a discernment process that "sees" God's will and results in the establishment of an appropriate and shared vision. Make no mistake, God is always the giver of the future. That is why people of faith live by hope. That is why the vision always transcends the present reality in which human beings strive to manage the given. Discernment is primarily a spiritual process, and leaders are used by God to guide the community in that endeavor.

In *The Once and Future Church*,[56] Loren B. Meade contends that the church now faces a major paradigm shift. Earlier models of understanding and being the church no longer are effective or appropriate. The world has changed, and God calls the church into a new paradigm. Visionary spiritual leaders will guide the church in discerning a definition of that new paradigm.

A Community Connecting Past and Future

Max Stackhouse writes about the need for a spirit-directed vision.

No civilization can endure for long if it is built on technological prowess, business acumen, political power, military might or mass-culture artistry only. It may well be that no civilization can exist without those things; but peace cannot be established on these bases alone, and none of these can, by themselves, discern truth or assure justice. The various sectors of society depend, in the long run, on a deeper foundation—a religious orientation. That is what forms the cognitive and emotive skeleton to which the deepest loyalties of the people adhere, and on which institutions depend.[57]

We bring to this moment in time the accumulated experience of a witnessing people. That past gives birth to tomorrow's vision. Faithful followers of Jesus in one generation plant the seeds of a new vision for the next. By engaging in the mission to which we are called in this moment, we are able to see Jesus walking on the water toward a new ministry.

Back in 1856, the California gold rush was slowing down, and many miners moved on to Nevada in search of silver. Two brothers from Pennsylvania staked themselves a claim and began with high hopes. It was nothing big, but with hard work they found enough to sustain them.

They heard about bigger and better silver strikes in the next valley. Figuring their own mine was about played out, they packed and moved on, wandering right out of history and into oblivion.

The deed to their silver mine traded hands several times. Eventually Henry Comstock bought the claim and, like others, was disappointed. The silver was all gone, but for some reason he continued to dig anyway. A few feet beyond the end of the abandoned tunnel, he hit one of the richest veins ever discovered. Earlier prospectors and miners had stopped only inches too soon, but Comstock found the "mother lode," turning this mine into a fabulous silver producer.

At the Iliff School of Theology commencement ceremonies in May of 1994, Randolph Nugent, general secretary of the United Methodist Board of Global Ministries, warned the graduates that they would be facing the "Peter Predicament." That is, as they try to give spiritual leadership in community transformation, they will face unending pleas for healing and never have in hand adequate resources to respond. The reference was to that occasion when the Apostle Peter, accompanied by John, was going to the temple to pray. Blocking their pathway to prayer was a disabled man who wanted a handout. In response, Peter said something like this: "I've got bad news and good news for you. The bad news is that I have no silver or gold to give. But the good news is that what I do have I will give to you. In the name of Jesus Christ of Nazareth, stand up and walk."[58]

Dr. Nugent went ahead to say to that class:

> Like Peter, your witness too, and in the name of healing, may take place in full recognition and awareness of crippled and crippling conditions: a social, political, and even religious climate of debilitating divisiveness and crippling alienation, hostility and fragmentation, both domestically and globally. . . . The vision of the global village connected by an information highway holds forth the promise of a human community harmoniously connected in cooperative interaction as never before. But the results seem to be more in the direction of increased fragmentation, isolation, and hostility.[59]

Spiritual visionaries never despair. They continue to dwell in the presence of the Almighty, waiting and listening, praying and searching the Scriptures. They trust that the future is safe within the hands of the God who created and is working still.

Localism and Globality

Two forces buffet leaders called to serve as visionaries. One is the movement toward localism; the other is the increasing globality of all life. No one can avoid the sheer reality of the latter. We live in a worldwide community where nothing is distant. Current transportation systems make it possible for us to travel to other cities in minutes or to other countries in a matter of hours. Magnificent communication systems enable us to talk with each other instantly, exchange written materials by fax, and even to see each other via video.

Global realities are now catching up with the vision given in the very first chapters of the Bible. The text declares that in the beginning, God created the earth and entrusted human beings with responsibility for its care. Now as never before it is possible to fulfill this commandment.

Those of us who follow Jesus Christ believe that God formed the Church for the sake of the entire earth. On the Day of Pentecost, the birthday of the church, a people long divided by language, nationality, and place were re-connected to each other by the fire of the Holy Spirit. If there is any organization that should be ready to live in a universal context, it is the Church.

Yet even as globality takes on more significance, so does particularity. The earth is populated by individuals who live most of their lives in specific places. Each person has value as one of sacred worth. Each person is endowed with freedom of choice to develop that value. The great cry arising in so many places is from individuals who want to be taken seriously, who want respect and appreciation.

Our culture overemphasizes individualism and large-scale organization. Exaggerated individualism leads persons to believe that they are self-sufficient and able to stand alone in life. Exaggerated emphasis on the whole leads to the belief that persons are not important or valuable. Life does not work when particularity or organization is carried to an extreme.

A local community provides a middle ground where persons may be appreciated and enabled to see larger human issues as well. The recovery of the local is one of the hallmarks of this generation. For Christians, the congregation provides a community that moves persons out of themselves. Within congregations, persons are nurtured in the spiritual disciplines of worship, prayer, and study. They also hear a common calling to serve neighbors in their community and the world. They receive God's vision for their group and for all of humankind.

Leadership Partners

Leadership is possible only in groups. Individuals need leaders when they come into relationship with others around a common vision and purpose. Leaders articulate goals worth pursuing. They inspire individuals and build a sense of community. However, individual leaders are most helpful to their community in teams.

"While much of the conventional wisdom about leadership seems to assume a leader working alone, the solo leader is rarely associated with effective leadership. Most effective leadership involves a number of people acting in a team relationship."[60]

Teams of leaders receive visions more clearly than individuals at any level. The membership of these teams must include both local and global leaders. People at the local level usually see that level better than those at the regional, national, or global level. However, their vision can be improved when coupled with the dreams of leaders responsible for seeing the larger scene.

As one set aside for regional leadership in an annual conference, I see myself as one member in a team of spiritual leaders. The other team members come from local settings. Individually and corporately, we listen to the Spirit and try to see the future which God is making known.

Within the team, others look to me for spiritual leadership. Building the team is more important that managing. This can be done by listening to persons and praying for them. Every day I work through pages of a prayer list in which I do just that. As a general superintendent, I also help my colleagues to appreciate their skills, and together we look for ways to grow and improve. Teamwork can be fostered through a pat on the back, a word of cheer, a feast in their honor, or assistance in defining their future and the future of the organization.[61]

The God who created the heavens and the earth is moving that universe into an unknown future. That is happening as communities at every level—local, regional and global—are being transformed into new organizations. God is using visionary spiritual leaders to guide and enable this transformation. The change may evoke our anxiety, but it also energizes our hopes.

One summer, my wife and I flew to the Pacific Northwest. Our flight took us directly over Mt. Saint Helens in Washington. The scene restored to memory those television images of the mountain literally blowing its top. From the air that half-sided peak still looked like a barren wasteland. The truth is that life is emerging from the ashes. In places where an animal left a print, algae is breaking through. On the lower part of the mountain side, fireweed, bracken, and thistle are growing. Lower still on the mountain, the fir, cottonwood, and alder have overcome the ashes.

In God's tomorrow there is a new heaven and a new earth. Right now that promise is alive in a vision. Spiritual leaders point to that vision and journey with all of God's people toward that hope.

Notes

1. W. Paul Jones, *Trumpet At Full Moon. An Introduction to Christian Spirituality as Diverse Practice* (Louisville: Westminster/John Knox Press, 1992), p. 7.
2. Henri J. M. Nouwen, *In the Name of Jesus* (New York: Crossroad, 1991), p. 25.
3. Ibid., pp. 29-30.
4. William R. Barr and Rena M. Yocom, *The Church in the Movement of the Spirit* (Grand Rapids: William B. Eerdmans Publishing Company, 1994), p. 1.
5. *Pulpit Digest*, January-February, 1986, p. 81.
6. Heather Murray Elkins, "Called by the Spirit, Heard in the Word," *New World Outlook*, January-February, 1993, p. 8.
7. Quoted by Leonard Sweet in *Quantum Spirituality* (Dayton: Whaleprints, 1991), pp. 196-97.
8. Roger K. Swanson and Shirley Clement, *The Faith-Sharing Congregation* (Nashville: Discipleship Resources, 1996), p. 85.
9. Sweet, *Quantum Spirituality*, pp. 198-99.
10. Charles R. Foster, *Educating Congregations: The Future of Christian Education* (Nashville: Abingdon Press, 1994), p. 13.
11. Sweet, *Quantum Spirituality*, p. 121.
12. Richard J. Foster, *Celebration of Discipline* (San Francisco: HarperCollins, 1988), pp. 62-76.
13. James MacGregor Burns, *Leadership* (New York: Harper & Row, 1978), p. 425.
14. Barbara S. Blaisdell, "A Downtown Church That Changed Its Tune," *The Christian Ministry*, November-December, 1994, p. 23.

15. *Foundations for Teaching and Learning in The United Methodist Church* (Nashville: Discipleship Resources, 1979), p. 66.
16. Blaisdell, *The Christian Mininstry*, p. 23.
17. Tom Sine, *Wild Hope* (Dallas: Word Publishing, 1991), p. 203.
18. Kenneth Leech, *The Eye of the Storm: Living Spiritually in the Real World* (New York: Harper San Francisco, 1992), p. 17.
19. William Stringfellow, *The Politics of Spirituality* (Philadelphia: Westminster Press, 1984), p. 19.
20. Eugene H. Peterson, *Working the Angles: The Shape of Pastoral Integrity* (Grand Rapids: William B. Eerdmans Publishing Company, 1987), p. 2.
21. Cf. Geoffrey Wainwright, *Doxology: The Praise of God in Worship, Doctrine and Life* (New York: Oxford University Press, 1980), pp. 37-44.
22. Ellen T. Charry, "Sacraments for the Christian Life," *The Christian Century*, November 15, 1995, p. 1,076.
23. D. H. Tripp, "Liturgy and Pastoral Service" in *The Study of Liturgy*, Cheslyn Jones, Geoffrey Wainwright and Edward Yarnold, SJ, eds. (New York: Oxford University Press, 1978), pp. 565-90.
24. Ibid., p. 579.
25. Ibid., pp. 576-77.
26. Ibid., p. 578.
27. *Quarterly Review*, Spring, 1983, p. 76.
28. Donald E. Messer, *Contemporary Images of Christian Ministry* (Nashville: Abingdon Press, 1989), p. 168.
29. Gerald Kennedy, *His Word Through Preaching* (New York: Harper & Brothers Publishers, 1947).
30. Halford E. Luccock, *In the Minister's Workshop* (New York-Nashville: Abingdon Press, 1944), p. 11.
31. Merrill R. Abbey, *The Word Interprets Us* (Nashville: Abingdon Press, 1967).
32. Walter C. Kaiser, Jr., "Leviticus," *The New Interpreter's Bible*, Volume I (Nashville: Abingdon Press, 1995), p. 1136.
33. Michael Eric Dyson, "Gardner Taylor: Poet Laureate of the Pulpit," *The Christian Century*, January 4-11, 1995, p. 16.
34. Alastair V. Campbell, *Rediscovering Pastoral Care* (Philadelphia: The Westminster Press, 1981), pp. 39-40.
35. Henri J. M. Nouwen, *The Wounded Healer* (New York: Doubleday/Image Books, 1972).
36. Quoted by Donald J. Shelby in a sermon, "Always on Call," October 23, 1994.
37. *The Book of Discipline of The United Methodist Church, 1996* (Nashville: The United Methodist Publishing House), Paragraph 104, p. 108.
38. Henri J. M. Nouwen, *Creative Ministry* (Garden City, N. Y.: Doubleday & Company, 1971), p. 70.

39. Ibid., pp. 77-87.
40. Lovett H. Weems, Jr., "Lead, Follow, or Be a Friend," *Circuit Rider*, April, 1995, p. 3.
41. Inagrace T. Dietterich, "Communal Decision-Making," *The Center Letter*, September, 1994.
42. Peter Block, *Stewardship* (San Francisco: Berrett-Koehler Publishers, 1993), p. 41.
43. Ibid.
44. William Abernethy, "The Man with the Muddy Shoes: The Sequel," *The Christian Ministry*, September-October, 1994, p. 16.
45. Darrell Jodock, "In Need of a Prophet," *The Christian Century*, January 18, 1995, p. 45.
46. Jim Wallis, *The Soul of Politics: A Practical and Prophetic Vision for Change* (The New Press and Orbis Books, 1994), p. xv.
47. Leech, *The Eye of the Storm*, p. 214.
48. D. B. Napier, "Prophet," *The Interpreter's Dictionary of the Bible* (Nashville: Abingdon Press, 1962), pp. 896, 910-19.
49. Donald E. Messer, *Contemporary Images of Christian Ministry* (Nashville: Abingdon Press, 1989), pp. 116-34.
50. From an unpublished paper by Phil Shull.
51. Mortimer Arias and Alan Johnson, *The Great Commission: Biblical Models for Evangelism* (Nashville: Abingdon Press, 1992), p. 84.
52. Leech, *The Eye of the Storm*, p. 216.
53. Lovett H. Weems, Jr., *Church Leadership* (Nashville: Abingdon Press, 1993), p. 37.
54. Ibid., p. 39.
55. Lovett H. Weems, Jr., *Church Leadership*, Fall, 1994, Vol. V, No. 1, p. 1.
56. Loren B. Meade, *The Once and Future Church: Reinventing the Congregation for a New Mission Frontier* (Washington, D.C.: The Alban Institute, 1993).
57. Max L. Stackhouse, "The Theological Challenge of Globalization," *The Christian Century*, May 3, 1989, p. 470.
58. Randolph Nugent, "In The Name Of Healing," *Mission Papers* (New York: Board of Global Ministries), July, 1994, p. 1.
59. Ibid., p. 2.
60. Weems, *Church Leadership*, pp. 69-70.
61. See John Cowan, *Sky*, March, 1994.